OVER THE WAVES

OVER THE WAVES

Poems of Encouragement, Prophecy and Worship

Mad Doodle

Grafted

Published in Great Britain by **Grafted**
www.graftedbydesign.co.uk
ISBN: 978-0-9562603-7-6

Before we begin, a plea from the author:

Do Not Take Offence

Do not take offence or think me holier than thou
I do not do or say these things to preen or take a bow
But since I see the inner me, I'm trying desperately
Not to be holier than anyone else, just holier than me.

I do not ask you to believe
This outer face trained to deceive
If you are to see what my faith is about
I'm reliant on Jesus to inside-me-out.

MAD-DOODLE'S INNER CHILD

Ephesians 6:13

Therefore put on the full armour of God, so that when the day of evil comes, you may be able to stand your ground, and after you have done everything, to stand.

Hebrews 12:1-3

Therefore, since we are surrounded by such a great cloud of witnesses, let us throw off everything that hinders and the sin that so easily entangles, and let us run with perseverance the race marked out for us.

Let us fix our eyes on Jesus, the author and perfecter of our faith, who for the joy set before him endured the cross, scorning its shame, and sat down at the right hand of the throne of God.

Consider him who endured such opposition from sinful men, so that you will not grow weary and lose heart.

INTRODUCTION

The poems in this book reflect twenty years of relationship with the Jesus of yesterday, today and forever. They look back to before I knew Him and forward to the days when we will meet face to face for the first time. But mostly they reflect my day to day life of living with, praying to and breathing in the God of Spirit who lives in me and changes me daily. Together we are working out my Salvation, sometimes closer to and sometimes further from the Me that He created me to be, but always growing through the experience of life.

Like the Psalmist I sometimes cry out in anguish and groan and hope for the new life of heaven. At other times I am overwhelmed by the recognition that I am loved by my Father, the Creator of the Universe, by His Word and Son, who came as a man and walked a long and lonely road to rescue me from the darkness of this world and by the Power of His Breath in me who seals me for His future kingdom and stands as my Protector in this one. Who that knows Him can cease from praising?

The psalmist speaks of a **SELAH** – a pause to reflect on the nature and the works of God. I hope that among these words will be something that will stimulate such a moment for you. And if any redirect you back to the spoken Word of God recorded in His testaments through His prophets, I hope you will read His Gospels and listen for His voice with a ready heart and a desire to go deeper, for it is in that internal space between heaven and earth that His voice becomes known to those who love Him, as sweet as a lover's kiss, or being wrapped in a Father's arms.

Do not be afraid to open your heart to Him – He is waiting and longing to hear from you. And His love is sufficient for every circumstance. Always remember that Love is the one thing that life and the Enemy cannot take from you. And Love is not weakness but the strength to endure and stand every flaw.

Whoever and wherever you are I pray His blessing for you.

Contents

My Quiet Time

In my quiet time
When I go into the half-light between worlds
And I'm cradled in the hand of God
And walking with my Lord
I can share the secrets of my secret soul
Without pretence, without deceit,
I can lay down by his feet
And open wide my suffering deep, and sin
And ask my Lord to come and enter in.

And he cleanses me,
He washes out my shadows and my shame, my guilt, my tears,
Turns my loneliness to love and calms my fears.
He empties me of anger, hate and fright,
He takes them on himself
And fills me up with joy and truth and light.
For he is my redeeming Lord, who's resting here with me,
And because I know he lives, I am set free;

Because I know he lives I am set free.

Majesty of Life

All praise, high and holy to thee, Majesty of life,
My master who became our servant king.
Without doubt I turn my face to thee
With trust I give my hand to thee
With love I give my soul to thee
To do with as you will.

Reach your hand into me and make me thine.
Place your purpose in my heart that I might know it as mine.
Guide me through the battle, Lord, and make my armour strong;
Walk beside me in the light that I may do no wrong.
When I fall from grace, please comfort me and bear my sin away;
Lead me out from darkest night into the light of day.
As a child I offer you my service, take me as I pray
And make of me a channel for thy might;
Lord, a channel make of me.

Quiet Moments

When I was a child, I listened as a child
But understood nothing of the words they said;
They spoke about a distant king who died to save us all
And though I thought it was a shame that he was dead
They couldn't make me see and they couldn't make me hear
For I closed my heart and mind to truth and light
'Cause it just seemed so unreal to me that such a man as this
Wouldn't be here now, defending truth and right.

Still, in quiet moments, when the nights are drawing in
And I feel the wind upon my face and the sunlight on my skin
I wonder at the majesty and miracle of it all
And the magnitude of Creation makes me feel so very small,
But small as I am, I begin to feel
His protection through each new day
And I'm learning, through love, just how much I could gain
Through talking to Him and walking in His way.

Living youth in pride, I everything denied;
I had to be the master of my soul and mind.
I needed proof for everything that ever came to light
Had but faith in me when no friend could I find.
He couldn't reach to me and he couldn't make me see
For in fear I closed my heart to trust and love,
For it just seemed so unreal to me that I could ever share
My loneliness and fears with one above.

Over The Waves

Now I start to see what the Lord can do for me
If I choose to set my foot upon the path He leads.
I think I start to know about the way that I went wrong
In thinking only of a truth in terms of deeds.
My eyes begin to open and my heart begins to feel
Though I'm still not very sure of where to go
But I'm reaching with my spirit now and reaching with my mind
And believe that someday soon I'll surely know.

Each man in his own heart must recognise the truth;
Each must learn to listen to the voice inside.
To each it is his own choice, no-one else can take away,
Only we can block it with our fear and pride.
Oh Lord help the world to know and Lord help the world to feel
The peace and love that only you can give
So that someday when we learn to know
The freedom of your truth
All Mankind will praise the Father that you live.

Altar of Love

When Time seems to stop and stare
And my heart is filled with bitterness and grief
And all things in this world seem to be unfair
When the dark clouds come and there's no one there
When the way seems barred with worry
And the spice is gone from life
And I'm reaching deep inside myself
To overcome the strife,
When it seems as if there's no way out,
My spirit's never going to rest again
When my fires are damped with emptiness,
Suppressed my soul with doubt and spiritual rain,

Then I lift my yearning spirit up to you Lord
Open up my emptiness and bitter pain
I lay myself an offering on your altar of Love
And take your restful arm to lift me high above
All the worries of the world and all my spiritual cares
To that zone of peace, the axis of eternity,
And you fill me up with bounteous gifts of laughter and of joy
And share with me your fatherhood, fraternity.
I long to drink in deeply of your peace bringing wine -
I come to you, I yield, make me thine.

Over The Waves

When shadows seem to fall upon my soul
And all people turn their backs and close their eyes
To the feelings deep inside fighting my control
When the cruel Fates seem against my every goal
When all peace seems defeated and frustration takes my hand
When the flames of desperation by my fear are fanned
When the demons' spears strike to my heart
Leave raw life's scars, my weaknesses and pain,
When time becomes my enemy
And shatters my illusions once again,

Then I lift my yearning spirit up to you Lord
Open up my emptiness and bitter pain
I lay myself an offering on your altar of Love
And take your restful arm to lift me high above
All the worries of the world and all my spiritual cares
To that zone of peace, the axis of eternity,
And you fill me up with bounteous gifts of laughter and of joy
And share with me your fatherhood, fraternity.
I long to drink in deeply of your peace bringing wine -
I come to you, I yield, make me thine.

Over The Waves

When night turns to day within my world
And the radiant light of sunshine glows inside
All the worries of the way are to the four winds hurled
And the flags upon my castle walls float free, unfurled,
When I'm reaching out for life and with peace I'm filled
When myself to me seems beautiful, my doubt distilled
When I'm walking three feet off the ground
And dances free my spirit in the sun,
And my happiness in light arrayed
Trips gently with the dance on feet of fun,

Then I lift my joy and peace back to you Lord,
Place my faith and hope into your hands.
I lay my love a gift upon your altar high
And walk with you in stillness 'neath a restful sky.
Bring back to you the wonder and the gentleness
That you've given me and shared through all eternity
And your worship echoes deep within my heart and soul
With the deep response I feel to your paternity.

I gave you all my shadows,
You redeemed them with your grace
You lifted me up high and let me look upon your face
I know how much it means to feel your spirit shining through
Take back my soul and help me be like you;
I'll try my best in service to be true.

The Follower

Dark, the streets are dark with hate
As he stumbles through the midst of mocks and jeers,
Upon his head a crown of pain
Bearing a burden not his own
But borne for those who jest and mock his tears.
Oh that I had the courage in me
To walk his side and approach with him
His lonely, empty, dirt-bedraggled death.

My eyes are upward drawn as they bind his tortured limbs
And the brutal iron pins the gentle hands
That smoothed the heads of children once,
That closed in praise and dignity
That broke his body, passed his blood
To we who would abandon him
Deny his truth, surrender him
With all too human weakness and despair.

The driving thuds of wood on iron resound
Buffeting and echoing through my head;
Though my hands close my ears
And my eyes are blind with tears
Each echoing stop to all our hopes
And dreams of things which might have been
Castigates our cowardice and shame
As, powerless, we watch upon his pain.

Over The Waves

Yet still he cries aloud not
Nor faints nor drops his gaze
But with a jaw fixed and a sweat-bespeckled brow
Turns heavenwards his anguished eyes
And prays through his despair
To the Father in whose hands he puts his soul.

With straining back and ropes unslack
They jolt him high until he falls
Restrained by tautened bonds upon his limbs
Which bearing his whole weight saw deep
And cut his battered shoulders to the raw.
Yet still he grits his teeth and holds his body high in agony
And racking shudders shake his fragile frame
As aching muscles seek to straight his back
Regain a fragment of control and ease of hurt.

And I turn my face away for I cannot watch the pain
And I cannot bear the shame it brings
To know that all stand by and make no move,
Not even we who call him Lord and know his name
And chose his way and walked his side until the test.
And I know as I pray with my eyes cast down
None else could bear his courage nor his crown.

Over The Waves

And he did it all for us
Can you see the blood and tears upon his brow?
Oh, how can it be that his pain and misery
Could free us from the bonds of sin
Could open up the doorway in
And rest our crying hearts therein -
He gave the very most he could afford
And my soul is washed clean by the blood and the tears of my
Lord.

Oh Lord My God and King

Oh, Lord, my God and King
Maker of everything,
Master of universes,
Father of Man,
All your great might and power
You laid aside that hour,
Left your bright home
For the dark world of men.

Broken from obedience,
Estranged from your beneficence,
We lived our lives alone
By sin defiled;
To seal that awful rift
Of sin, you gave the gift
Of your great majesty
In the heart of a child.

Oh, what a sacrifice
To submit to that awful price;
The child of pure innocence
Came to us to die.
Now from his home above
Flows his great depth of love,
Shines his pure radiance
Lifted on high.

The Nativity

Scene 1 – the Birth

Narrator: The Emperor Augustus ordered a census to be taken throughout the Roman Empire.

Augustus: Take a census throughout the Empire

Narrator: When this first census took place, Quirinius was the governor of Syria.

Quirinius: Well ... go on ... count them!

Narrator: Everyone went to register himself, each to his own town.

All change places

Narrator: Joseph went from the town of Nazareth in Galilee to the town of Bethlehem in Judea, the birthplace of King David.

Joseph enters – walks to Bethlehem.

Narrator: Joseph went there because he was a descendant of David.

Joseph preens.

Narrator: He went to register with Mary who was promised in marriage to him.

Joseph looks round then rushes back to Nazareth to fetch Mary.

Narrator: She was pregnant.

A cushion is thrown from the wings and Mary pushes it in her robe.

Over The Waves

Narrator: While they were in Bethlehem the time came for her to have her baby, but there was no room for them to stay at the inn.

All the rest huddle together in a group. One opens the door to Joseph.

Innkeeper: Sorry. No room.

He shuts the door. Joseph tries to knock again. Mary taps him on the shoulder. He stands in front of her with his cloak spread.

Narrator: She gave birth to her first son, wrapped him in strips of cloth and laid him in a manger.

The manger creates itself and she lays the baby in it. Joseph goes back to the door.

Joseph : Do you have any hot water?

Scene 2 – The Shepherds

Narrator: There were shepherds living out in the fields near Bethlehem, keeping watch over their flocks by night.

The three shepherds are sitting playing cards.

Shepherd 3: I'll see ewe and raise ewe five.

Shepherd 1: You're trying to pull the wool over my eyes.

Shepherd 2: I think you're both baa-rmy. I fold.

Voices are heard offstage.

Angel: Excuse me, have you seen three shepherds?

Basil: Baaaah!

Angel: Thank you Basil.

He walks over and stands behind the concentrating shepherds. The other angels form in a line behind him.

Narrator: An angel of the Lord appeared to them and the glory of the Lord shone around them.

Angel: Erm. Excuse me.

The shepherds drop their cards in surprise.

Narrator: And they were terrified.

The shepherds look at each other, shrug and cower.

Narrator: But the angel said to them.

Angel: Do not be afraid.

They all look happy again.

Angel: I bring you good news of great joy which will be for all the people.

Shepherd 2: What about the sheep?

Angel: ... for all the people!

Over The Waves

Shepherd 2 shrugs.

Angel: Today in the town of David, a saviour has been born to you; he is Christ the Lord. This will be a sign for you: you will find the baby wrapped in cloths and lying in a manger.

Shepherd 1: Oh, yes! The King of Creation in a cattle stall. Ha Ha!

Shepherd 3: Did Uncle Harry put you up to this?

Narrator: Suddenly a great company of the heavenly host appeared with the angel singing Glory to God.

Host pop out from behind the angel.

Host: Glory! Glory!

They shuffle into a row and recite from bits of paper. The angel conducts.

Host: Glory to God in the highest and on earth peace to all on whom his favour rests.

Narrator: When the angels had left them ...

The angels run away.

Narrator : ... and gone into heaven. The shepherds said to one another ...

Shepherd 1: Let us go to Bethlehem and see this thing that has happened, which the Lord has told us about.

He exits.

Shepherd 2: Can I bring my sheep?

He follows

Shepherd 2: Come on Basil.

Shepherd 3 goes to the table and looks at Shepherd 1's cards.

Over The Waves

Shepherd 3: Three kings.

He looks at the sky

Shepherd 3: Thank you Lord.

He exits

Narrator: So they hurried off and found Mary and Joseph and the baby, who was lying in the manger.

Stable, manger Mary & Joseph reform and the shepherds kneel.

Narrator: When they had seen him they spread the word concerning what had been told them about this child, and all who heard were amazed by what the shepherds said to them.

The shepherds rush to speak to their friends.

Shepherd 1: Have you heard the one about the angels, the baby and the manger. It's a Christmas cracker.

Shepherd 3: Well, Rachael, there was this shining man in a nightie ...

Narrator: The shepherds returned glorifying and praising God for all the things they had heard and seen.

The shepherds return to their places and sit down to sleep.

Shepherd 3: Goodnight Basil.

Basil: (Offstage) Baaaah!

Scene 3 – The Magi

Narrator: After Jesus was born in Bethlehem in Judaea, during the time of King Herod, magi from the east came to Jerusalem and asked ...

The wise men enter following the star and kneel to Herod.

Magi: Where is he who has been born king of the Jews. We saw his star in the east and have come to worship him.

Herod paces up and down angrily.

Narrator: When King Herod heard this he was disturbed ...

Herod: Oh drat! (He throws down his crown)

Narrator: And all Jerusalem with him ...

All: Oh drat! (*Throw something down*)

Narrator: When he had called together all the people's chief priests and teachers of the law, he asked them where the Christ was to be born.

Herod: Where is the Christ child to be born?

Priest: In Bethlehem in Judaea.

Teacher: For this is what the prophet has written ...

He takes out a book and reads.

> But you oh Bethlehem in the land of Judah
> Are by no means least among the rulers of Judah
> For out of you will come a ruler
> Who will be the shepherd of my people Israel.

Herod: I knew that. I was just testing you.

Narrator: Then Herod called the Magi secretly and found out from them the exact time the star had appeared.

Over The Waves

Magi 1 looks at his watch, Magi 2 takes out his diary, Magi 3 looks at the sky.

Herod: Well?

Magi 1: Two years last Thursday.

Herod: Go and make a careful search for the child. As soon as you can find him report to me so that I too may go and worship him. (*Aside*) Brooo ha ha ha!

He rubs his hands. Everyone hisses.

Narrator: After they had heard the king. They went on their way and the star they had seen in the east went ahead of them until it stopped over the place where the child was.

The Magi enter following the star. The stable reforms. Mary and Joseph enter.

Narrator: When they saw the star they were overjoyed.

Magi 2: What joy!

Narrator: On coming to the house they saw the child with his mother Mary, and they bowed down and worshiped him.

Magi bow.

Narrator: Then they opened their treasures and presented him with gifts of gold and of incense and of myrrh.

Magi pull gifts from about their persons.

Narrator: And having been warned in a dream not to go back to Herod, they returned to their country by another route.

Magi 1: If I were you I would take a long vacation.

Magi 2: Somewhere well off the beaten track.

Magi 3: Egypt's nice this time of year.

The Magi exit followed by Joseph and Mary.

Over The Waves

Soldiers rush onto the set and search it. They find nothing and return to Herod.

Herod: OH DRAT!!

He throws his crown down again.

Herod: I want my Mummy!

He sucks his thumb.

His Steps

I will walk in the steps of the God whom I love
And though shadows abound around me
And though Death calls my name, I will not be afraid
For the power of the Lord has unbound me.
The invincible Death has been conquered by Love
He has no authority on me
And I will place all my trust in my Father above
And the gift of grace He's poured out upon me.

He is my Saviour;
He is my King;
All Creation His holy praises sing.
He is the Lord of Eternity -
The Alpha and Omega, He,
And yet He gave His life for me
On Calvary's tree,
Oh the sacrifice and pain
Yet he rose up again
And released the grip of Death upon my soul.
Through the sadness and the tears
The darkness of all these years
The Love of my Lord Jesus keeps me whole.

Over The Waves

God gave all Men the gift of immeasurable worth
In the shape of the Son He'd begotten
But as time passes by, in our sinfulness and pride
The sacrifice he made is forgotten.
It is for us who believe, who from Death are reprieved
To awake the hearts of those who have fallen
Reach out and touch their shuttered minds,
Break down each barrier that binds
Help them hear the voice of Him who is calling.

God has promised us life; God has promised us truth
And the promises He makes are eternal
And our spirits he lifts with innumerable gifts
Pours out on us his loving paternal.
His Spirit in us stirs up a fountain of joy
And revokes the dark with which we're surrounded
And I long for the day when we can meet face to face
And this love burning in me is unbounded.

Still My Anxious Heart

Still my anxious heart, Lord
And calm my restless mind
Fill me up with patience
And strength that I may find
All my tears and sadness
Drifting far away
Knowing you can give me strength
To make it through the day.

When my spirit's low and shadows
Darken all around
Open up my ears to hear
The deep enthralling sound
Of the quiet voice that stills me
Gives me peace of mind
Leads me gently through the dark
And leaves my fears behind.

Take my part when evil spirits
Start to bring me down.
Softly let your flowing peace
Ease away my frown
When I seek to hide from you
And bar your cleansing flame,
Help me yield my castle walls
And trust your love again.

Over The Waves

I beg of you my Saviour King
Who suffered pain for me.
Help me to be willing, Lord
To be what I should be;
Let my eyes see clearly
Where my feet should tread.
Help me yield my self-love
And accept my daily bread.

Till, O Lord, upon me
You turn the final page;
End my tribulation
And free me from the cage
Of my earthbound service
And through your endless grace
Renew my tarnished spirit
And meet me face to face.

In Heaven's holy place
I'll meet my Saviour face to face.

We'll Do the Best We Can

All around the world, Lord, there are children on the run
Running from they know not what, to where they do not know
Something in their broken lives has driven them to fly
To seek a place, a time where they can grow.

Help them find a home in you, Lord;
Let them see the way is clear;
Let them know you in their darkest hour.
Like birds in winter who lose their way
Searching for a brighter day
Find them a place to rest their feet
And close their tired wings in sleep.
Hear their lonely voices as they pray,
Lord, give them peace and take their cares away.

All around the world are people searching for a home
Trapped in worlds of darkness, living futureless and lost
In cardboard boxes, under bridges, open doorways, parks
Looking back on broken bridges crossed.

Over The Waves

Help them find a place to live, Lord
Even if they will not hear;
They are still your children and in need.
Like sheep in winter who lose their way
Lost in the night and far away
Guide their steps towards the fold
And bring them in from winter's cold.
Hear their empty voices as they call,
For, Lord, you gave up your life to save them all.

All around the world are people reaching out to you,
Giving up a past of sin forgiven by your love.
Help us give our lives to help the ones who still are lost
Put their faith in Thee and God above.

Help us help their lonely lives, Lord
Hear me as I pray to you;
Use us here on earth to do your will
Like flowers after winter's night
Our hearts are open to Thy light;
Lead us to our serving place
And through us share your holy grace.
Give us what it is we have to do;
We'll do the best we can with help from you.

All Joy and Glory

All joy and glory to the world
A King is born today;
He comes to heal our broken days,
To fill our lives with gifts and praise.
O Child of radiant bliss,
You gave your life for this.

Though born in poverty, His dignity
And grace are shining through;
Great men upon his presence stand
The stars have led by his command
With gifts of precious worth
To dignify his birth.

And shepherds from the darkened fields
Have placed their lambs on trust
Into the hands of guardians bright
And make their way by black of night
To worship by his feet
God incarnate to greet.

They look upon his majesty
In innocence enthroned;
With joyful hearts they celebrate,
They have not learned his earthly fate
But welcome the child adored
Our once eternal Lord.

Over The Waves

Come all you children, sad and lost
To meet the holy child
None can explain until you find
The way to him the peace of mind
Surpassing everything
That knowing him can bring.

The General

A child is born in Bethlehem
Long prophesied, he comes to heal
To walk the same path that you and I walk
To share what we see, share what we feel
He takes his awesome weight of power
And lays it off to wear a robe
Of all the patterns of pure humanity
That he wove for us and we betrayed.

*And his star shines brightly
In the depth of the heavens
And our hearts are filled with joy
And the angel praises
Echo though the ages
He is born!*

His life he leads to serve his father
A channel for the Spirit's might,
A touch of heaven in the lives of sinners
Who come in faith to his holy Word
To breach the wound 'twixt Man and God
He lays his life, a bridge of power
Comes through the dark clouds of sin and suffering
Sends forth his Spirit to lead us home.

Over The Waves

And his star shines brightly
In the depth of the heavens
And our hearts are filled with joy
And the angel praises
Echo though the ages
He's alive!

And now God's army await their General
To march beside them in the fight
And Man must choose now or die forever -
March with Jesus; break Satan's might.
The time draws near, the final battle,
All Heaven waits; all earth attends
And the signs they prophesied us
Show that Jesus will soon be here.

And his star shines brightly
In the depth of the heavens
And our hearts are filled with joy
And the angel praises
Echo though the ages
He's alive!
He's alive!
Christ Arise!

Dear Lord and Father

Dear Lord and Father of Mankind
It's in you that my constancy I find
Without you there's a shadow on my mind
Lord and Father.
You came into my hiding place;
You let me look upon your face;
You filled my heart and mind with grace
And I'm forgiven.
Time passes and the world changes;
Each minute and each second brings a moving tide
Of sensory perceptions, fragile moments, fleeting dreams
And sugared voices seeking to misguide.

The way darkens and the night grows colder;
The chill winds of despair attend my every strife.
Each daring step of courage seems to falter, if I fail
To hold your guiding light within my life.

The gates to the city are my destination;
On my back, I carry all my guilt and shame.
I may not bear it inward; I yield it at your word
And cry aloud the password, Jesus' name.

Throughout life's journey, you've been my mentor;
My Self you've borne complete above the tide of doubt.
I could not walk the waves alone without your helping hand
Through you my sin is washed completely out.

The Seekers

The Peace Seeker

Journey-worn and weary,
I looked through disillusioned eyes,
My heart forlorn and fearing
Ideals suppressed by compromise,
Pretending, inventing,
A stranger in the world's disguise
Reaching without counting cost
And conscience-torn I paid the price.
Fragmented dreams that once burned bright
Came flooding through my mind at night;
In scattered shards my spirit lay
With memories of broken yesterdays
And sad parades of burnt out sorrow
Bore visions of a dark tomorrow;
In inward grief I did not hear
The words you spoke to calm my fear.

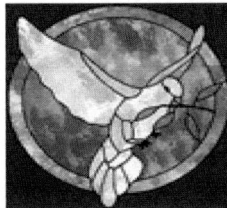

Over The Waves

And you said :

Peace, perfect peace of the Father, be with you;
Joy, perfect joy of the Spirit, be in you;
Love, perfect love of the Son, let it heal you;
Be what I meant you to be.
When the peace of the Father is within you,
When the joy of the Spirit is in your heart,
When the love of the Son is your guide and friend,
Then I'll pour power through you,
Give you gifts without end.

Let me heal the broken places in your heart and mind and soul;
Accept the price I paid to make you whole.

The Joy Seeker

Uncaring in my freedom,
I filled my life with being Me;
I could not spare the time
To see the others not so free,
Unresting and seeking
The things put there for only me,
Escaping from my emptiness
I thought that pleasure was the key.
Yet underneath, so empty still
That hollow feeling naught could fill;
In ever speeding circles, I
Was drawn into the cyclone's eye;
Whilst parties, presents, money, friends
Around me fell to bitter ends,
I closed my eyes to all the pain
And blocked your voice out once again.

But you said : (Chorus)

33

The Love Seeker

Bitter, hurt and heart-bruised
I'd take once more my hope in hand
In doubt and so confused
With fear I couldn't understand,
A yearning, so burning,
And by my desperation fanned,
In trembling hope that finally
My feelings weren't on shifting sand.
In adoration watching on
While they my torture smiled upon,
I'd feel once more the crushing blow
And bitterness would inward grow;
So torn within and feeling small
I'd turn my face back to the wall
And wouldn't hear the words you spoke
Through thinking how my heart was broke.

But you said : (Chorus)

The Power Seeker

Filled with greed and hunger
From years of insecurities
And being long held under
By human spite and bigotries,
By Fortune's chance
From shame and poverty reprieved,
The need to scrape and crawl was gone;
I'd do exactly as I pleased.
In my new-found strength I'd seek
To see their faults, to find the weak
And damaged places in their lives
And in them I'd start twisting knives.
In power games and lies and jests
I'd watch them fall and come out best.
I'd never yield a precious hour
Of being strong – for promised power.

But you said : (Chorus)

The Truth Seeker

Once I felt the needs of Man
And lived my life through day by day
In grim determination
To hold his precious love at bay.
Cleansed, renewed
My load of care now washed away
I kneel beneath my Saviour's grace
And walk upon a bright new way.
To one I once knew wasn't there
I open now my heart in prayer;
To fight this bitter world of sin
I ask his gentle presence in.
His promised gifts of peace and love
And joy and power flow from above.
This bright new spirit born in me -
He gave his life to let it be set free.

And he said : (Chorus)

Do Not Be Afraid

Do not be afraid!
Walk out in my holy name,
Though you may be tossed in the wind and storm,
Know the wind is the wind of My Spirit
Which sweeps away the clouds of doubt,
And the storms are My storms of righteousness
Which wash out the sins of your fears.
Stand upright in the winds and I will uphold you;
With your face to the storm I will unfold to you
All the wonders of My Grace.
Know I am with you in the darkest moments,
Never resting in My protection,
Never stinting in my gifts
Of power, strength and joy.
Ever merciful, ever bountiful,

Over The Waves

I am the omniscient, omnipresent God of all Creation.
Let your heart tremble with awe for My Majesty.
But let not that awe become terror,
For I am Infinite Mercy to those who love Me
And Infinite Love to those who call upon my name.
Know I am your Father who provides for you so much more
Than you can ever begin to comprehend.
Close your eyes and touch that never-ending fountain
Of joy, love and hope
That springs eternally from the depths of My Spirit,
To burn in fire and glory in the depths of your own.
Let my light burn in your heart till it speaks out
In tongues of fire, in words of strength and mystery
Or words in tune with My Creation.
Let the truth of the Spirit speak with your lips
And with your eyes and with your hands.

Over The Waves

Live My Word – let your being be a living testament
To the truth of My being.
Let the world see in your lives the life of the one
I sent to save you from the just penalties of Death.
Through you they can see into the heart of My Beloved Son
Which echoes its perfection in your lives -
Do not be afraid to open your hearts and pour out
The endless praise which ever flows through the halls of your
mind -
You have seen and felt and heard – and you have believed -
Will they not understand also
If you only show them the fullness of your heart
And speak with the voice of My Son to the emptiness in theirs?
Be all I meant you to be, for only in this can you be
My messengers to a yearning lonely world.
I am placing a drought of understanding in the hearts of the lost
Of the lonely, of the sure and unsure.
Let the water of My Spirit flowing through the springs of your
hearts
Bring life to the desert – light in the darkness.
Be not afraid for I will never yield you in the battle -
Only keep your eyes on He who walks before you and beside you
And ever turn your faces to the mercy of your just and loving
God
And the world will never know a time more filled
With truth and righteousness and praise.
Again I say – fear not the enemy
For his end is in my plan – while the Children of My Spirit
Will never fail.

Sending Out

When you're far away
From all the things you've ever known,
If the night seems darker
When you're out there on your own,
If anything seems harder
When there's no one else to share
Just recall I'm waiting
And if you'll only stop and turn to me
I am there.

I'll be with you in the darkest night;
Trust my peace to ease your pain.
Give me all your hurts and weariness;
Let me free your thoughts again.
Close your eyes and sleep within my love
As you touch me with your prayer
I'll be with you till the morning light;
Just call my name and I'll be there.

Over The Waves

I will bring you friends,
Bonds of new found loyalties.
All your waking hours
Filled with peace and joy will be.
Though you may feel weary
Under Labour's heavy care
Just recall that I'm with you
And if you'll only stop and turn to me
I am there.

I'll be with you on the hardest path,
Shoulder all your heavy loads,
Through all the mire of doubts and fears
Walk with you on endless roads.
When you stand amidst my enemies,
Should they laugh and make you small,
Take my hands that broke and bled for you
And with my words we'll change them all.

Just remember, child,
All the promises that I have made;
Of the things that Earth owns,
You have no need to be afraid.
Walk my path with courage;
Take the things I've planned for you.
Know I'm there beside you
And through all dark and dangers
I'll be true.

Over The Waves

Now be my lantern in the darkest night;
Show the World my endless love.
Be the symbol of my sacrifice;
Show them life is not enough.
As my Spirit shines out from your eyes
They will see their Saviour's face.
Let me use your eyes and voice and hands
To lead my lost ones back to grace.

The Tongues of Men and Angels

Sometimes, Dear Lord, my heart is so full
of love and praise that I cannot say;
and sometimes, Lord, the world seems so hard
to understand and I cannot pray.
What can I do when you show me a friend
who needs my prayer in unknowable ways?
How do I speak out the words of life that bring
healing and harmony, happiness and grace.

Father give me a special voice
To talk to you like the angels do.
Jesus, teach me new songs of praise
That I might draw near to you.

Lord, use my mind as your writing pad
for powerful words you want to be prayed;
And Lord, use my heart as your easel frame
to paint the pictures you want displayed;
Lord use my life as a portrait of you
to show your presence in all my ways;
Lord use my voice to sing simple songs,
prayers of power, prophecy and praise.

Over The Waves

Forgive me, Lord, when I try too hard
to get things right and instead I fail.
Help me to hear your promise and plan;
Within my life let your will prevail.
Open my mind to understand
Your secret prayers released from above
Teach me to listen and echo your voice to bring
Learning and leadership, light and life and love.

God's Hug Song

When I'm alone and sad or afraid
And no one seems to care;
When there seems no answer to the prayers I've prayed
And I just need a hug but there's nobody there
I take my Bible from the shelf
Read of how you died in pain
And remember that you promised me
I need never feel alone again.

And the Holy Spirit hugs me inside-out
And my precious Jesus hugs me outside-in
And God enfolds the whole with his Father-love
So I'm loved by three for the price of one
When I know that God sent His only son
To set my spirit free
And bring eternal life.

The Son of Life came to touch our hearts
To free us from our pain.
He called to his children who were lost and alone
To open their hearts to His love again.
He cried to the Father to forgive our sins
With his last and dying breath,
Then opened wide his arms of love
And hugged this world to death.

Over The Waves

Jesus calls us now to be his arms
Where no one seems to care
To be the answer to the prayers they pray
And to bring his love in everywhere.
We are His Word in the eyes of the lost
With His Spirit breath inside;
Jesus, through us, heals their suffering
And dries the tears they've cried.

On The Kingdom Green

Everybody's somebody's neighbour
On the Kingdom Village Green
All together worshipping the Saviour
With our hearts and hands made clean.

Jesus died upon the Cross
To free us from our sin.
God cleans us from the inside out
And pours his Spirit in.

So we should learn to love the World
Like Jesus did before.
Your neighbour cannot run from God
When Jesus lives next door.

When his Spirit lives next door
In You and Me !!

Wave Makers

It's time to take action! It's time to make waves!
It's time to put our trust in the ruler who saves!
It's time to break strongholds in the fight against sin
With God's armour on the outside and the Spirit within.

We're children of God; we have been chosen
To speak out His words in a world lost in fear.
We stand up in His name with our Spirits unbroken
And speak of his Salvation to all who will hear.

It's time to take action ...

We're soldiers of Heaven; we have a mission
Given by the one whose holy death was our birth.
We stand up to be counted , without division
As witnesses of Jesus to the ends of the earth.

Father God, strong to save
Send your power like a tidal wave.
Help us raise up holy breakers
'Cause we wanna be your movers and shakers.

Precious Jesus, make us new;
Change our hearts to be like you.
Plant your Word and let it grow
So we can stand against the flow.

Over The Waves

With our families and friends,
Help us set up Kingdom trends.
Let the Light of Life shine through
Winning hearts and minds to you.

Holy Spirit, hear our call;
By your presence change us all.
Send us out to win the nation
'Cause we wanna be your wave generation.

It's time to take action ...

We ain't going to hide or run from the fight
'Cause we are Heaven's victors in the Kingdom of light!

Surf's up!

Cobblestones and Cornerstones

Cobblestones and cornerstones -
Help us know the difference, Lord
Cornerstones not cobblestones
Is what you've called us to be.

If I cause my friend to trip,
I make your Kingdom weak,
But if I build his spirit up
Your presence he will seek.

If I go my own way,
No one will see your face
But if your Spirit lives in me
The world will see your grace.

Teach me not to judge my friend
And think my ways are best.
Only you know how each heart
Will answer every test.

Help me Lord to serve you
With all my heart and mind.
Show the world, within my life
The Temple you designed.

Three Guiding Lights

Lord, be my light in your harbour;
Guide me to your throne.
Lord, place your compass inside me;
Make my ways your own.
Be my anchor when the waves ride high
And I'm lost in the winds and the darkening sky,
With the sail of your Spirit
And your Word as my keel
I'll come sailing home.

The Word of God

In the darkness before time began
You laid your perfect plan
For the route by which your perfect will
Would lead the heart of Man.
You sent your Son to show the Way
Of sacrifice and love
So lead me onward every day
Let your Word be my beacon from above.

Over The Waves

The Witness of the Spirit

Touch my heart with deeper knowledge
To make the choice within.
Be the Captain of my worldly voyage
To bring your Kingdom in.
Strengthen me when I grow weak
And darkness starts to prey;
Show me now your deeper wisdom
As your Spirit illuminates my way.

The Circumstances

Steer me through your purposes
Upon life's stormy sea;
Navigate me through the rocks, to where
My serving place should be.
Give me from your grace the courage
To face each challenge through;
Make your time and need my vision;
Let your World be my lantern guiding true.

52

Lord, Give me Words to Pray the Prayer

Lord take me where you want me
Just don't leave me here
Imprisoned by my inward doubt
A captive of my fear.
Oh Lord, you know I fear to touch
The Grace that makes me free
Lest I discover loneliness
The deepest part of me.

My heart has always yearned the touch
That makes my soul complete.
My head knows that I'll only find it
Here at Jesus's feet
But fear and doubt ring me about,
I'd rather hide than learn
That only under grace I lack
The love for which I yearn.

I know you and I've known your touch
But now my Spirit's dry
And I'm afraid to lose control
Lest all my truth's a lie.
I've never fully dared your love
It now seems far away
I'd give my all to trust you
And remember how to pray.

Over The Waves

I doubt myself, my motives
And I can't accept my worth
Despite your endless sacrifice
Despite my second birth.
Though times I've turned my face to meet
Your patient gaze above
It's still easier to run away
Than run towards your love.

I know I am a child of God
I know my Saviour's grace
I've felt your Spirit in my life
I've sought your hidden face.
Lord, help me through the tides of doubt
To live for you alone.
Lord, fill with all your bounteous grace
This poor child that you own.

O make me see, oh help me hear
Your soft and gentle voice
When all around the Enemy prowls
With self condemning noise.
You died to free me from the dark,
My ransomed soul to win
You wrote your truth upon my heart
And cleansed me from my sin.

Over The Waves

So help me throw aside the chains
And claim the promise made
When you bled on the Cross for me
And said the price was paid.
Lord, change me from this broken child
Still hiding from your sight;
Break loose the bonds of law and guilt
And let me shine your light.

The time's too late for hiding;
There's too much left to do
My task's awaiting only me -
I have to see it through,
But I must claim the holy blood
You yielded to atone
Before I feel your Spirit's touch
And know I'm not alone.

Lord, help me grasp the love within
That I have never known
And help me yield my wayward heart
To live for you alone.
Without your presence and your touch
My Father, Brother, Friend,
My Saviour, King and Counsellor
My loss would know no end.

Over The Waves

Lord give me words to pray the prayer
That frees me in your sight;
Lord help me share the inner Me;
Please hold my Spirit tight.
Surround me with the love with which
You patiently attend
And let me fully, deep and free
Accept my true heart's friend.

Faithful Pebbles

Lord, you chose a man called Simon
You named him Peter the rock
You said you could build your church upon his faith
And you placed him in charge of your flock
Lord I want to be a believer
Won't you change my heart of stone
I want to be the rock from which you can build your church
With Jesus as my cornerstone

You sent John to baptise in the Jordan
Proclaiming to the lost of Israel
But the ripples went out to the ends of the earth
And touched the lives of others as well
Lord I want to be your disciple
Now you've set my spirit free
I want to be a pebble in the pond of the people I know
With Jesus spreading out from me.

Over The Waves

You sent your son, a sacrifice, to save us
A shepherd for the lost and the weak
He laid down his life as a foundation stone
Your word in flesh for sinners who seek
Lord I want to serve you like Jesus
Show me how to take up my cross
Because you pebble-dashed the world with your stones of faith
So you could build your holy church on us.
Build your holy church...
Build your holy church...
Build your holy church on us!

Everybody's Different

Everybody's different
But we are all the same
When we stand before the Saviour
And we call upon his name.
He's chosen you and me to spread
The good news of His love
And when it gets too difficult
He helps us from above.
So everybody Praise the Lord
With heart and hands and voice
And as we share His Kingdom love
The angels will rejoice.
Oh my Saviour, you gave your life for me
When you took my sin upon your head
And died on Calvary's tree.
Oh my Father, I give my life to you
And you'll lead me through the darkness
With your Spirit shining through.

Father's Eyes

Look beyond the outside
To the face of the Father's child within
See the risen Lord's beloved
Though their face be shamed and scarred with sin
If their soul is seeking heaven
Their past can be made clean
Lord, give to us your Spirit's eyes
And let us see the good you've seen.

For the world that we live in
Is not all that it seems
And it's hard to see beyond the scars
To people's cares and dreams.
Those we recognise as failures
In the fallen world's disguise
Could be prophets for the Kingdom
If we look through Father's eyes.

Look beyond the mocking
To the face of the Father's child within
The beloved of the Holy One
Though his face be shamed and scarred with sin
Each wound that we've inflicted
Upon His brow he bears
And the Father tears his eyes away
To wash the nations with His tears.

Over The Waves

So suffer the little children
As they leave the darkness for the light
For time has been their torment
And each heart is wounded by the fight
Feel the deep compassion
Which wells up through the living Lord within
Let their eyes see only Jesus' face
Through love their healing now begin.

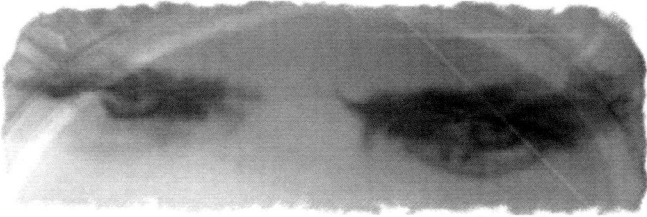

Faithful Servant

You have been my servant
Faithful for so long
You are my voice to many
In you they see my light

Though times you may be weary
You've never turned aside
From the tasks I've laid your hand to
And the path I've laid before.

I have seen your struggles
Been there when times were hard
Together we have conquered
When you have trusted in my Love.

Listen as I whisper now
Words into your prayer
An answer for your searching heart
A comfort in your fear

Submit your all to inward love
And answer to my call
Each daily step you take with me
Brings my Heaven to the world

Over The Waves

Breathe deeply of my Kingdom Love
Lay aside your worldly pain
Oh my son you are as gold to me
Believe and doubt not you are loved

So the world will see your tenderness
And learn My love through your embrace
O Child of God be all you can in me
Be loved and love and live as mine

What's between our hearts will never end
None can gauge such depth of love
You've chosen Me and I have chosen You
You are in Me; I am in You.

Ideas from Psalm 61

Hear my voice Most High:
The cry of supplication from the depth of my being,
A heart that yearns, that burns to be yours.
From the oppression of my heart I turn my need to you;
From my frailty and lostness, draw me into your steadfast love;
From the shadows I cast my weakness upon your strength.

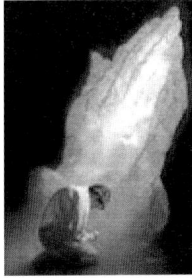

You are my centre:
You cradle me safe from those who would harm me,
Concealed in the haven of your heart.
Let eternity find me in your presence;
Entrench and enfold me in your everlasting security.

How can I grasp it?

The Holy One receives my meagre commitment
And pours on me from His heaven the store of wonders
Reserved for those whose dependence is on His Name.

Over The Waves

Majesty, when our King comes to us
Add to Him age upon age, new birth upon new birth,
From time to time everlasting through the centuries.
Give Him the hearts of the ages; turn all searching eyes to Him.

May He be for all time entwined and infused in Your Glory,
A reflection of the perfection of Your Grace.
May powers of Goodness attend Him and defend Him,
Raise holy shields of righteousness over His throne.

Lord, make this humble heart your Holy-of-Holies,
That moment-by-moment its beating cadence may echo
The praises and promises eternally due
To your ineffable, holy and everlasting Name.

Mephibosheth

There was a young man named Mephibosheth
Who was kept from the King by a shibboleth
As the royal court drew near, he trembled with fear
For he thought that he faced a terrible death.

Well the poor little lad wasn't able
And thus met the King quite unstable
David said, "Do not fear, for your Pa was so dear
That I want you to eat at my table.

(This poem was a challenge set to find a limerick rhyme for Mephibosheth. He was the grandson of David's enemy Saul, and also was crippled in an accident when escaping from David. David's court had a saying (also known as a shibboleth) that the lame may not enter the King's court. David ignored the saying because he loved Mephibosheth's father Jonathan, and Mephibosheth was invited to eat at the King's table).

66

The Challenge

Can't you feel the darkness looming?
Don't you fear the fires of Hell?
Don't you know that the Deceiver
And the reaver of souls is nigh?
In the shadows he is scheming,
While Heaven's warriors lie dreaming,
Seducing My heart's treasure
To lives of sloth and leisure
As on troubled Earth unfold
His plans to tarnish Heaven's gold.

But a time it is coming and the time has now come
When the Children of my Spirit must worship as one.
Renew your zeal and ardour from my surfeit above
Let the oil of my Spirit fuel the lamp of your love

Be vigil! Watchmen do not slumber,
For my sheep have wandered far
Into the realm of the Accuser
And the abuser of truth and light.
His twisted truths they have accepted
While my true life they have rejected.
How can they make their choices
If you stand with silenced voices?
Serve me now with opened eyes;
Live to reveal the Devil's lies.

Over The Waves

Keep your eyes fixed on Jesus as you wait for the day
As darkness falls upon the earth I call you now to pray
Be my Word and my Witness, be my Light and my Love
And with your lives come worship me in Spirit and truth.

Over The Waves

Awake O Church, while you were sleeping
Dissent and doubting have crept in
Have your stagnant hearts stopped beating;
Is he defeating you by his lies.
Cast off the heavy chains that bound you
Accept the radiant life that found you
Abandoning your rivalry
Weep tears of true revival.
Set aside your earthly pride
And seize the truth for which Love died.

With a breastplate of righteousness and a buckler of truth
And feet shod with willingness to spread the good news
Wear the helmet of Salvation; wield the Spirit's sword
And extinguish Satan's arrows with Faith's shield and the Word.

Over The Waves

Though the Judgement day approaches
And the wolf is at the door,
When the heat of battle rages
The courageous will be secure.
Do not doubt your faith and calling
When the flames of night start falling
It is my heart's desire
To snatch you from the fire;
Be assured my outstretched arm
Will keep my loved ones safe from harm.

Do not flinch or flee the danger; don't you know I'm by your side
The power of heaven is moving; My love will not be denied
The enemy will scatter as you enter the strife
And your valiant souls are reborn to the Kingdom of Life...

Your valiant souls are reborn to the Kingdom of Life...

Your valiant souls are reborn to
the Kingdom of Life!

Glory

I fall before your Glory
I kneel beneath the fountain of your grace
Your mercy rains upon me
Oh Holy Lamb of God.

You are my beginning and my end
All I am, will ever be
Is in your grasp
You've cleansed my past
And my future is in your hands
Your Love means all my world to me
I bow in worship at your feet
Enthralled in wonder
Rapt in praise
I yield to you my all.

Over The Waves

Occupy my senses
Let my world be bound within your grasp
Till Kingdom Love consumes me
Oh Holy Lamb of God.

You are my Redeemer and my Lord
I turn to you from all my sin
And selfish gain
You bore my blame
And my blood is upon your hands.
My heart gained freedom through your love
To serve your will through endless days
Reveal to my
Enraptured soul
The glory of your ways.

"God is a Spirit and they that worship Him must worship Him in spirit and in truth."

John 4:24

The Wheel of Fire

Yahweh -> Yeshua

I am waiting
Anticipating
The presence of the Lord Most High
The Holy One.

He draws me nearer
I see Him clearer
Above His head the angels sing
Their songs of ardent praise
Crying "Holy Holy is the Lord
The Ancient of Days"

I see Him on His throne of gold
Sapphire beneath his feet
Yet on his palms are wounds of old
That made my life complete.

Oh holy, all-redeeming Lord
I fall before your throne
And I worship you alone.

Yeshua -> Ruach

I fall before Him
And adore Him
The ever-living Son of Man
The righteous King

Who brought salvation
And restoration
Now glorified at God's right hand
He daily intercedes
To win the crown of life for those
For whom He pleads

His loving arms enfold each child
Repentant and sincere
And fills with light their darkened lives
And calms their worldly fear

Oh holy, all-empowering God
I fall before your throne
And I worship you alone.

Ruach -> Yahweh

I can but praise Him
His Spirit blazing
Streams Heaven through the hearts of those
He calls His Saints

Cast all before Him
And implore Him
To change from glory into glory
Your shamed humanity
As all within you makes the choice
That sets you free

And ever-living love itself
From deep within Him pours
As the voice of His Creation song
Like mighty waters roars

Oh holy all-creating Lord
I fall before your throne
And I worship you alone.

Trinity

My heart is trembling
With never-ending
Devotion to the eternal Lord
Who reigns on High

With reveration
And jubilation
In righteous robes the multitudes
Cry "Holy is the Lamb!"
And fall before the presence of
The great I AM.

Behold the Lord, the Lamb, the Life
In perfect unity
The triune presence of the One
Who breathed life into me

Oh holy one and only God
I fall before your throne
And I worship you alone

When?

When will it be
The day of grace
When Heaven falls upon the earth
And your righteous name
Will be proclaimed
By every man
In every land?
When will it be
The King of Kings
Will walk among us once again
And His glorious face
And His wondrous grace
Shall be revealed to all men?
When will it be?
When will it be?

Like a thief in the night he will come to the world;
Are you ready to fall before His throne?
Has he entered your name in the Lamb's book of life?
You are lost if your name is not known.

Over The Waves

When will it be
That judgment comes
Like sudden lightning from the sky
And all wickedness
Will be swept away
By Heaven's fire
From on high?
When will it be
Your justice reigns
And darkness flees from every part
And the tyrants' crowns
Will be cast down
And you will raise the pure in heart?
When will it be?
When will it be?

And Your peace it will reign in the Kingdom of Love
And the wolf with the lamb will be free
For the earth will be full of the knowledge of You
As the waters they cover the sea.

Over The Waves

When will it be
The Son of Man
Descends from Heaven on the clouds
And His angel train
Exalt His name
And all the nations praise out loud?
When will it be
The end decreed
Will pour upon us like a flood
As You call the blessed
To eternal rest
Saved and ransomed by your blood?
When will it be?
When will it be?

And the nations will tremble and mourn as they see
The sign of the Son in the sky
But the righteous will shine like the stars in the heavens
Raised from dust to your glory on High.

Over The Waves

When will it be
The golden streets
Are laid at last on Zion's height
And the city waits
With wide open gates
Your faithful remnant clothed in white?
When will it be
You claim with joy
Your place within her very heart
And dry up her tears
From the barren years
Your purified
And chosen Bride?
When will it be?
When will it be?

He who testifies to these things says
"Yes I am coming soon!"
Amen! Come Lord Jesus!
Come Lord Jesus!
Come Lord Jesus! - Amen!

Precious One

Precious one
Bend your ear to my voice
Do not worry – you are close to my heart
I have set My hand upon My plough
And guide it with My perfect will
And your name is blessed by angels
As they watch you on your way.

Be renewed
As I pour out My love
Designed to meet and fill your every need
I have worked your life into My plan
Let My purpose be your fire still
Take My hand and walk beside Me
As with childlike faith you pray.

Be released
As I claim you as My own
And My vision forms the pattern for your life
Do not fear to walk the road ahead
Jus follow closely in My steps
Oh Child of faith stay faithful
As you seek me on your way.

Over The Waves

I am here
As close as if I held you
Drink deeply from the wellspring of My life
I will never now release the hold
I have upon your heart and mind
As you serve My heart's desire
And you win My children home.

Be wise and holy
Bear My thoughts in all you do
My love will live and shine within your life
Draw closer and receive My will
Accept your weakness – draw My strength
Forever I'll be closer than a breath
I'll hold your spirit close
through life and death.

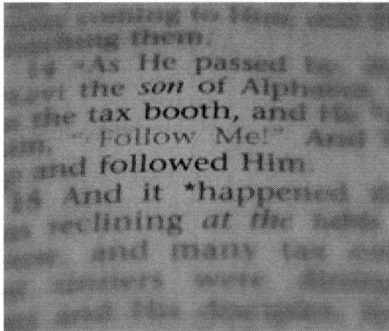

Unchosen

Unchosen, unloved and unlovable,
A child of tears in a place of darkness
Unable to know love
To accept truth
A broken image of a reality ever out of reach.

Lead me to a point of knowing!
Teach my heart to believe
That someone, somewhere someday
Could choose to see beyond
The papered cracks of my existence,
Could want to know this lost child.

Where is the worth? - Why this hunger?
Why this solitary yearning
To be part of something more?

Why is His love not enough?

Is there nothing in this lost spirit
That touches another heart
In friendship, in love, in choice?

You are so far out of reach
I can't find you in the darkness!

Over The Waves

I cannot accept that You could choose me
Because no one does
No one can
No one will.

If I speak to others of my lostness
Then all that they give becomes worthless
For if I have asked
The choosing is not of their hearts
And I am not chosen but pitied,
Just as in knowing that You reach out
To even the most worthless
I find no worth for me in You.

Who will acknowledge my spirit?
Who will be my friend in the dark place
To lead me out of despair?

Tomorrow the pain will sink back
Beneath the waves into the lonely dark
Tomorrow the light will shine
But tonight is so alone
And it is always there
That looming lurking image of doubt
The Enemy's hand in spiritual defeat
My spiritual surrender.

How can I claim Him
When I feel unchosen
Broken lost afraid?

Over The Waves

How can I trust when all I am is alone
Living in an identity given by others -
Fractured in spirit – oppressed by doubt.

Do you see me?
Do you know me?
Can anyone see into who I am?

I return again to the point of loss
Knowing only You can save me
But unable to reach out,
Riding the tides of worthlessness
Swept in by the winds of rejection.

We were not made to be lonely -
How can I be so lost in the crowd,
How can they not see me?

Oh for the dawn when I can be Me again
Sure in my own confidence and my Self
Free from the lostness of the dark
When I accept my life on the outside
Knowing intimacy cannot be mine.
Lord, help me to lay aside this daily seeking -
Seeking acceptance, friendship
And the acknowledgement of my inner heart.

Why have you made me this person?

Over The Waves

If I am to be ever-lone
Then give me a heart that does not seek
In my humanity
Another heart's acceptance.

I don't want to be alone
But if this is what you have planned
For my life
That I should be an outsider to the end
Then change my heart to acceptance -
Let me be satisfied in you alone.

Don't let me doubt you
For your plan is my only foundation.
Without you, what remains?
To walk alone
Until darkness comes.

Oh Lord, by day I see the path
But by night I need your light.
Don't leave me here;
Take my hand -
Give me your peace by still waters.

**Psalm 22, Psalm 139, Psalm 25:16-18,
Psalm 27:7-10, Psalm 27:13-14
Psalm 28:6-9**

Friendship Prayer

Oh Lord,
I pray for his happiness,
That all your promises will meet
And be fulfilled in his life.
I pray for his peace in despair -
His certainty in doubt -
His growing closer to you day by day.
I pray for his health and happiness -
That you will guide his choices
And stand by him in his dark times.

Give him friends to hold him
When the clouds roll in
And love to sustain him
Against all calamity.
Rejoice in his joy
Let angels watch over his every step.
Protect and uphold him against the evil one.
He is truly yours
And I bless him in your presence
And I thank you for his time
In my time of need.

Gethsemane - Chosen to choose

Father now the darkness falls
My heart is weak my mind afraid.
How can I walk this path you've set
Before my eyes?
Pity now my dark despair;
Remove this cup, this hour forswear.
My burdened soul is grieved to death;
The end draws near

**The road to life must lead through
The coldness of the grave
And with reluctant feet I tread
This darkened way.**

Over The Waves

I need you, your strength Lord,
I cannot stand.
Enfold me; uphold me
Within your hand.
Oh Father, I'm falling;
I cannot see
Beyond this dark vision
That tortures me.

Your distant promised glory
Casts the shadow of a tree
Where I must face the punishment
To set Men free.
Have I the courage in me
To walk this road alone,
To pain and separation
As I have never known?

Over The Waves

Your will it is hard Lord;
Must I embrace
This vision you've shown me
Of my disgrace?
I see their cruel faces;
I feel their wounds.
The lostness of millions
For whom I choose.

The darkness consumes me;
Lord send your light.
Oh angel, stoop closer
Restore my strength.
My God you have answered;
The choice is made.
It will be completed
Thy will be done.

Over The Waves

I will drain this poisoned cup;
It's bitter dregs, my destiny,
And I will walk into Your storm,
My head held high.
Fix my eyes on Heaven's reward;
my heart upon the truth of your Word.
In Mercy's steps, Lord, guide my feet
To Calvary.

I need you, your strength Lord,
I cannot stand.
Enfold me; uphold me
Within your hand.
My God you have answered;
the choice is made.
It will be completed;
Thy will be done.

Father now the darkness falls.
Lord, Thy will be done.

Rooted

I'm rooted in Jesus
I'm rooted in Jesus
I'm rooted in Jesus
I'm rooted and established in Love

His love is wider than the widest sea
And deeper than the heart of Me
It's longer than the lengths of Time
And higher than my hopes can climb.
More than I can know
It helps my Spirit grow
God's Love will never from me part
It's high, wide, long, deep in my heart.

I'm rooted, rooted, rooted, rooted,
Rooted and established in
Love.

Precious Child

Precious Child,
Let your racing heart be still
As you're reaching out with all your strength
To find My perfect will.
Let your heart and mind and soul
Be intertwined in mine, made whole.
Though the night seems dark and lonely, when you pray
Heaven's love is but a beating heart away.

Precious Child,
Rest your head against my chest
As you're pressing in with all your strength
Your hunger will be blessed.
Let your heart and mind and soul
Be intertwined in mine, made whole.
When the journey's weary troubles cloud your day,
Heaven's peace is but a breath of prayer away

Precious Child,
Take my hands and let me guide
As your simple steps of faith and trust
Awake a Father's pride.
Let your heart and mind and soul
Be intertwined in mine, made whole.
As my angels guard your every step in love
Heaven's power waits but a feathers breadth above.

Over The Waves

Though the road seems hard and paved with pain
As you stumble in the way,
I'll lift you in my arms again,
Only turn to me and pray.
Set aside those things the world desires,
Heaven's riches I'll impart.
Let my truest love restore your soul,
Burn with fire in your heart.

Precious Child,
Take the hand I reach to you.
Walk the bridge of hope into the arms
Of One who bled for you.
Let your heart and mind and soul
Be intertwined in mine, made whole.
All eternity is yours - just walk my way -
Heaven's grace flows, through the choice you make today.

The Persecution Rap

The Roman Procurator

I am the very model of a Roman Procurator
And if you fall into my hands you're most unfortunat-e;
For Christian your survival rate is very much against the odds
Unless you turn away from Christ and sacrifice to pagan gods.
I do not care how innocent the practice of your faith may be;
You do not fit into my world or live by my philosophy
So I will take your children's heads
and slaughter you without reprieve
Because I do not understand the mystery that you believe.

The Christian Martyrs

We won't recant and we won't turn
Though we're crushed and beaten, bleed and burn
We take our cross and follow Him
Who faced this punishment for our sin
Hang us by our thumbs with weights
Stretch us over burning grates
Tear our flesh and throw us to the beasts
But we have a future at the angels' feasts.

Over The Waves

The Chief Witchfinder General

I am the very model of a Chief Witchfinder General;
I'll put you in my dock although the charges be ephemeral.
The evidence may be trumped up
and witnesses may have no proof
But you'll be branded as the Devil's spawn
no matter what the truth.
The only way to prove that there has been a terrible mistake
Is sit upon a ducking stool and be plunged in the village lake
And if you drown your innocence
will be by all the world proclaimed
And if you don't you'll be tied to a stake and on a pyre inflamed.

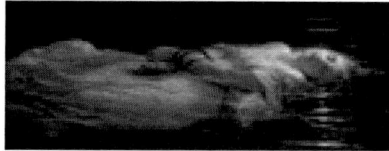

The Victims

How can you claim to follow Him
Injustice follows your every whim?
Where he would fight to win a soul,
Death and destruction is your goal.
Unnumbered people lost from grace
Look on you and see the Devil's face
At Heaven's gate you'll receive your lot
When God declares, "I knew you not!"

Over The Waves

The Catholic Crusader

I am the very model of a Catholic Crusader
On a mission to eliminate the infidel invader
And on my way I'll stop off, to burn and kill and persecute
And fill my coffers with a mighty plethora of stolen loot.
The Holy Pope has promised to eternally forgive my sin
If I the Holy City from the evil of the pagans win
So do not worry if I pillage, torture, rape and slaughter you
It's all in a good cause and something
all good Christians ought to do.

The Other Faiths

We won't believe, we've seen your ways
And we turn our backs on the God you praise
You prove your God by how you live
And what you've done we can't forgive
Destroy and torture as you will
Steal and lie, blaspheme and kill
You've had your way now count the cost
To the King of Kings for the lives you've lost.

Over The Waves

The Spanish Chief Inquisitor

I am the very model of a Spanish Chief Inquisitor;
My torture chamber has a new device for every visitor
And if you won't reveal the truth I'll only have to guess the lot
And snap your toes and fingers
till you break down and confess the lot.
Your neighbour may accuse you of a crime which is heretical;
I'll throw you in my prison cell, however hypothetical.
I have no toleration for a different ideology;
My eyes are blinded to the gaping holes in my theology.

The Faithful

Through troubled days we make our stand
For the King who sits at God's right hand
Slaves of darkness may have their way
But we believe in a brighter day.
God's Holy Spirit protects our soul
Through pain and suffering will keep us whole
Our broken bodies will be restored
For we belong to the living Lord.

*Considering our history (you do not have
to search at all)
It's really quite amazing
there's the remnant of a church at all.*

Letters To Caiaphas

- SIMEON - A scribe
- CAIAPHAS - The High Priest

Scene comes up on CAIAPHAS sat at a table with a large needle sewing together a large curtain which has been torn down the middle.

SIMEON, a scribe enters, with two letters, looking rather distraught. CAIAPHAS beckons him over.

CAIAPHAS : You're late! - and what's the matter? You look like you've just seen a ghost.

SIMEON : I wish I had. Life would be much more simple. I've just been having a little chat with my father.

CAIAPHAS : Your father? Didn't he ...?

SIMEON : Yes. A week ago last Thursday. He had all the works - nice new tomb, best linen, costly ointment, obituary in hatches, matches & dispatches. It took most of my inheritance to pay for it & he's a bit ticked off about that.

CAIAPHAS : *<Confused>* Yes?

SIMEON : He's not too happy about the house being demolished in yesterday's earthquake either.

CAIAPHAS : *<Dazed>* He just told you this?

Over The Waves

SIMEON : Yes. I met him in the temple courts. He and his 'friends'. I think Lazarus is arranging an 'after-death' holy knees-up. Sounds like every-body who was any-body will be there. I guess it's a sort of wake for the awake.

CAIAPHAS : That earthquake did some very strange things.

SIMEON : Yes, I heard about the temple curtain. < *He indicates - there is a short silence* > Did you ever think we might have been wrong?

CAIAPHAS : What?

SIMEON : Well, you know, the sky turning black, and the earth shaking and the dead rising - it's not your normal Passover, is it.

CAIAPHAS : He had to die. He was trouble.

SIMEON : But didn't we say that only God's Messiah could do the things he did - long before he did them.

CAIAPHAS : That's academic. He broke the law - he couldn't be the Messiah.

SIMEON : Yes, of course - that was it. So which of Moses laws was it that he broke?

CAIAPHAS : Moses laws?

SIMEON : Yes.

Over The Waves

CAIAPHAS : Well, I can't put my finger on a specific one, but he definitely didn't agree with our understanding of how the Law was to be interpreted.

SIMEON : So it was politics really.

CAIAPHAS : No. The man was obviously possessed.

SIMEON : But surely the demons all acknowledged him as the Son of God and fled from him.

CAIAPHAS : Stage managed. < *A long pause* > Definitely. < *They both contemplate* >

SIMEON : You know, he did say he would rise again.

CAIAPHAS : Well let's make sure he can't stage manage that one. Organise for Centurion Septimus to put a guard on the tomb, to stop his disciples from stealing the body and pretending he's back.

SIMEON : Septimus isn't available. I've just had a letter from him saying he's had a religious conversion. He says he thinks Jesus was the Son of ... < *he looks at CAIAPHAS' face* > ... it doesn't matter.

CAIAPHAS : Get Gaius Decius then.

SIMEON : I've got a letter from him too. He says he won't do anything else for us until we pay him the 300 denarii it cost to straighten out their breastplates after last night.

CAIAPHAS : What?

Over The Waves

SIMEON : Well apparently, when they went to Gethsemane to arrest the ... the ... *< he gives up trying to think of another word for Messiah >* they all fell flat on their faces in the dirt. Gaius Decius says they've had to replace all their breastplates and it will take weeks to get the scratches out.

CAIAPHAS : But we need those soldiers to guard the tomb. Very well, you'd better get the money from the treasury. Now tell Pilate ...

< Fade out & Black out >

Scene opens on CAIAPHAS looking out over the audience as if through a window on the fourth wall. He is looking down, examining the latest work on the temple courts and seems mightily pleased. SIMEON enters.

CAIAPHAS : It's coming on well, don't you think. They'll be finished lining the inner walls of the courtyard soon and can start on the inlaid gold. After 30 yrs of planning, things are finally beginning to come together.

SIMEON takes a brief look out of the window and answers distractedly.

SIMEON : Yes. There's a problem.

CAIAPHAS : What is it ?

SIMEON : I've just had a report from Gaius Decius.

CAIAPHAS : And...?

Over The Waves

SIMEON : He says you owe him another 300 denarii.

CAIAPHAS : < *a pause* > Don't tell me - the body's gone.

SIMEON : Uhuh.

CAIAPHAS : I suppose it's too much to hope that it was buried in this morning's earthquake.

SIMEON : Uhuh.

CAIAPHAS : Let me guess - he's walking around, large as life in the temple courts.

SIMEON : Not exactly. It's rumoured that he's encountered some women and his disciples, but no-one else appears to have seen him.

CAIAPHAS : Good. Good. We might be able to work with this after all. Women and peasants make very poor witnesses, and the soldiers can be bought off. Take a press release Simeon - now how shall we put this ...

< Fade out & Black out >

CAIAPHAS & SIMEON enter

CAIAPHAS : Well, at least we know what they've been up to for the last 50 days.

SIMEON : You don't find it rather peculiar that they could learn all those languages in such a short time?

Over The Waves

CAIAPHAS : All it takes is a little application. I myself speak three languages fluently.

SIMEON : But you said it yourself - Jesus' disciples are peasants. And there's no such thing as a crash course in Phrygian. Besides which, I was there - I heard them in Aramaic, but I spoke to those round me and they swore they heard the same words in dozens of different languages.

CAIAPHAS : Coincidence. They were drunk and babbling gibberish - people heard what they wanted to hear.

SIMEON : And what about the tongues of fire that rested on each of them?

CAIAPHAS : I must admit, the flaming hairdos were a neat trick. I must ask them how they did that.

SIMEON : And the wind that filled the temple, was that a trick too?

CAIAPHAS : I begin to wonder about you Simeon. You're not starting to believe all this nonsense are you?

SIMEON : No, but I know three thousand who do.

< Fade out & Black out >

SIMEON enters with another letter.

CAIAPHAS : Who's that from?

SIMEON : Saul.

Over The Waves

CAIAPHAS : Ah good, news from Damascus. How's my favourite persecutor getting on?

SIMEON : Well...?

CAIAPHAS : Good. Good. Are the prisons filling up then?

SIMEON : Not exactly.

CAIAPHAS : What's he been doing all this time then?

SIMEON : Preaching.

CAIAPHAS : I didn't send him there to give a sermon.

SIMEON : No. Well, apparently he had a change of heart on the way.

CAIAPHAS : What do you mean a change of heart?

SIMEON : *< reading from the letter >* Apparently, he was on the road to Damascus, and a bright light flashed from heaven and Jesus spoke to him.

CAIAPHAS : He saw Jesus? It was really him?

SIMEON : Well, no. He was blinded by the light, and fell to the ground.

CAIAPHAS : And the men with him? What did they see?

SIMEON : Nothing. They just heard someone speaking to Saul.

Over The Waves

CAIAPHAS : So someone flashes a light in Saul's eyes and shouts "Hey I'm Jesus" and Saul decides to throw up his whole life on the spot?

SIMEON : Well, not quite. He was blinded for three days and then a man came who said Jesus had sent him, and prayed for him and something like scales fell off his eyes.

CAIAPHAS : Well, it all sounds very fishy to me.

SIMEON : Anyway, he's changed his name to Paul and now he's busy preaching the good news to everybody.

CAIAPHAS : The what!

SIMEON : The goo... the... the terrible fiction about the Messi... em... the Son of G... em...

CAIAPHAS : I'm definitely beginning to worry about you Simeon.

Black out . CAIAPHAS leaves the stage. Lights come up on SIMEON reading his own letter to CAIAPHAS.

Over The Waves

Dear Caiaphas

I don't know how this will find you or even if it will find you still alive. I don't want to say "He told you so!" but do you remember when Jesus spoke about the Temple and said not one stone would be left on another. He also said that when we saw the day approaching, the believers should flee to the hills and not even stop to return to their homes. So that's what we did when we saw the Romans approaching. I hear that the Roman commander gave instructions that the temple was not to be destroyed, after all, it was only completed four years ago, but the soldiers ran riot and set fire to the cedar-wood lining of those walls of which you were so proud. All the golden inlay melted and ran between the stones, and they had to dismantle it stone by stone to recover it. And so, not one stone was left as Jesus said. If he was right about that, I wonder just how much else he was right about - and I often wonder how much you really knew about who He was when you ordered his death. And all in the name of peace. Was it worth it, do you think?

Lights fade to black out.

You Are The Centre

You are the centre of my worship,
You are the source from which I breathe.
In You my restless heart is founded –
I long to touch your heart of grace.

Your never-ending song of mercy
revives the broken life in me.
In You I rest in sweet surrender –
You touch my soul with eternal joy.

You are the Love of my life –
Your tender touch
Soothes me in my pain.
You are the Lord of my heart,
renewing my worth
as I trust in you again.

Over The Waves

You shepherd me through tears and laughter,
my will enfolded in Your peace,
Your Word the hope to guide my searching,
Your quiet whisper my heart's release.

I seek the stillness of Your waters,
beneath the shelter of your wing,
fathom deep in true submission,
Your arms of mercy rescue me.

You are the Love of my life –
Your tender touch
Soothes me in my pain.
You are the Lord of my heart,
renewing my worth
as I trust in you again.

He leadeth me beside the still waters.

Roll back the Jordan

Roll back the Jordan
We're entering the promised land
Roll back the Jordan
We're crossing through on the sand
Roll back the Jordan
The people of Israel are home
God's rolling back the Jordan today
And we're on our way.

Roll back the Jordan
God's covenant is leading the way
Roll back the Jordan
He's called out a people who pray
Roll back the Jordan
We'll make his name worshiped abroad
Who's rolling back the Jordan today
Is our living Lord.

Come to the Jordan
Prepare ye the way of the Lord
Come to the Jordan
His summons cannot be ignored
Come to the Jordan
God's Covenant's still leading today
He's rolling back Death's Jordan in triumph
And we're on our way.

From Prisoner to Prism

As those pills in your hand you are shaking,
please remember whose heart you are breaking.
You think all hope is lost
but remember the cost,
for this life is not yours for the taking.

If all you recall is heart-broken
and it seems Joy has never been woken,
life seems barren and grey
and you fear the new day
with its pains and its cruel words spoken,

though in deep desperation you wallow
and your Spirit's foundation seems hollow,
let Hope be your guide
to a Peace deep inside
and a spiritual path you must follow.

You cannot believe Love waits for you;
the words of the priests used to bore you.
but God's Word is true -
He longs to know you
and He'll never despise or ignore you.

Over The Waves

On the door of your heart He is knocking;
will you open to Him, just stop blocking
and turn from your sin -
when you welcome him in
you will find Pain's dark prison unlocking.

The chains of the past cannot hold you
when arms of true heart-love enfold you.
Oh Friend, do not fear
but only draw near
for no Dark from His Light can withhold you.

Our Lord paid dear blood for Salvation;
through His death we now have new creation.
Brother, join us in light,
step away from the night
and in His Life claim true restoration.

All our lives are now interconnected,
Since the Son was from death resurrected.
Where lost hearts do not know,
Our task is to show
The image of His love reflected.

There are aspects of God's rainbow light
That can only be seen through your plight;
Broken lives in their need
May be touched and be freed
If you do not succumb or take flight.

Over The Waves

So resist Night's sweet calling. Resist!
From God's plan you would be sorely missed.
Child, receive tender Grace
And let shine from your face
A life which the Father has kissed.

O Word of Ancient Mystery

O Word of ancient mystery, the Beginning and the End,
the breath that caused this fragile earth to live,
you stepped right into History to become a sinner's friend
and you gave till there was nothing left to give.
I wonder, in the garden, did you think about the loss,
the cost to save humanity from sin
and I wonder did you question, as you hung upon the cross,
just what it took, my ransomed soul to win.

For yours is a prodigal love;
you lavish from above
the surfeit of your hand
on this dry and faith-lorn land.
You exchanged heaven's gold
for the lives that we had sold
now our reddest sins are covered by
the white of purest, prodigal love.

114

Over The Waves

The depth of the atonement that you made there at the last
is immeasurable to one so poor as I,
that you gambled all the Kingdom when a single life was cast
into a sinful world, in purity to die.
Here I kneel in awe and wonder, as I contemplate the grace...
perceiving death, the Son of Man obeys.
Through the liberal blood you shed there, you unshackled
Death's embrace;
now my living heart is given to your praise.

For yours is a prodigal love;
you lavish from above
the surfeit of your hand
on this dry and faith-lorn land.
You exchanged heaven's gold
for the lives that we had sold
now our reddest sins are covered by
the white of purest, prodigal love.

It's Got To Rain

It's got to rain, Oh my Lord, it's got to rain!
Lord on our hope-thirsting land, please come again.
Let true revival flow till all the people know.
It's got to rain, Oh my Lord, it's got to rain!

It's got to pour, Oh my Lord, it's got to pour!
From heaven's store, King of Life, please send us more.
Your mercy from above, revealing all your love.
It's got to pour, Oh my Lord, it's got to pour!

You've got to flame, Oh my Lord, you've got to flame
Into the hearts of your people once again
until with lives ablaze the world will sing your praise.
You've got to flame, Oh my Lord, you've got to flame!

It's got to rain, Oh my Lord, it's got to rain!
It's got to pour, Oh my Lord, it's got to pour!
You've got to flame, Oh my Lord, you've got to flame!
It's got to rain, Oh my Lord, it's got to rain!

The Church was Born for Healing

The Church was born for healing of the nations,
to create disciples, teach and to baptise,
joining hearts and minds across the generations,
standing for our God against the Devil's lies.
But where once we shared around one loving table,
our fickle hearts learned swiftly to despise...
over rubble from the broken walls of Babel
we would babble, without hope of compromise.

Could we lay aside our pride,
standing side by side,
we could show a world that doesn't care
the love of one who died,
sweeping years of guilt away
that anchored hurts of yesterday,
to restore to life the temple that He built
for a better way.

Over The Waves

So the sources that we sprang from long forgotten,
and the courses that we wended far behind
now we're flowing here united as one river
with the Spirit of a holy God entwined.
Unlimited, we answer to one calling;
with urgent hearts, to save the lost we flood
and the bastions of our ancient hates are falling
as insurgent grace ignites our common blood.

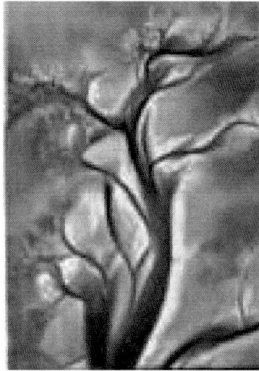

Do you feel the rising tide,
that cannot be denied?
Break down the barricades that keep
you from your brothers' side?
For the day of streams is gone,
we are become a swelling throng
arising now with heart and mind and soul
to the Saviour's song.

Spirit of the Father

Spirit of the Father, be the firth in my heart,
    where the river of my spirit
    is mingled with the start
    of an ocean that's unbounded,
    a love that's fathom-founded,
    a grace that can't be sounded,
    where your life suffuses mine.

I want to be where I cannot tell
just where it is I end and You begin,
in the sea, where by sapphire shores
the curling waves of joy swell up within;
away from the limits of my earth-bound life,
to taste the salty wind and feel the rising tide,
inner-whelmed by the mystery of knowing You
as I surrender my heartbeat
to the rhythm that you keep
where your deep cries out to deep
so deep inside.

The Ten Laws That God Gave

The first rule that God gave to help us live our lives :
>1   **Worship the Lord alone.**

The **second** rule that God gave to help us live our lives :
>2   **Don't bow down to idols**
>1   And worship the Lord alone.

The **third** rule that God gave to help us live our lives :
>3   **Use God's name well**
>2   Don't bow down to idols
>1   (And) worship the Lord alone.

The **fourth** rule that God gave to help us live our lives :
>4   **Keep the Sabbath holy**
>3   Use God's name well
>2   Don't bow down to idols
>1   (And) worship the Lord alone.

The **fifth** rule that God gave to help us live our lives :
>5   **Honour your folks**
>4   Keep the Sabbath holy
>3   Use God's name well
>2   Don't bow down to idols
>1   (And) worship the Lord alone.

Over The Waves

The **sixth** rule that God gave to help us live our lives :
  6 **Don't kill through hating**
  5 Honour your folks
  4 Keep the Sabbath holy
  3 Use God's name well
  2 Don't bow down to idols
  1 (And) worship the Lord alone.

The **seventh** rule that God gave to help us live our lives :
  7 **Keep your wedding promise**
  6 Don't kill through hating
  5 Honour your folks
  4 Keep the Sabbath holy
  3 Use God's name well
  2 Don't bow down to idols
  1 (And) worship the Lord alone.

The **eighth** rule that God gave to help us live our lives :
  8 **Don't take what's not yours**
  7 Keep your wedding promise
  6 Don't kill through hating
  5 Honour your folks
  4 Keep the Sabbath holy
  3 Use God's name well
  2 Don't bow down to idols
  1 (And) worship the Lord alone.

Over The Waves

The **ninth** rule that God gave to help us live our lives :
9 **Be a truthful witness**
8 Don't take what's not yours
7 Keep your wedding promise
6 Don't kill through hating
5 Honour your folks
4 Keep the Sabbath holy
3 Use God's name well
2 Don't bow down to idols
1 (And) worship the Lord alone.

The **tenth** rule that God gave to help us live our lives :
10 **Don't want what you don't have**
9 Be a truthful witness
8 Don't take what's not yours
7 Keep your wedding promise
6 Don't kill through hating
5 Honour your folks
4 Keep the Sabbath holy
3 Use God's name well
2 Don't bow down to idols
1 (And) worship the Lord alone.

The Ten Commandments Today

Chorus

God wrote his laws down on tablets of stone
then Jesus came to earth to show us how
Now His Holy Spirit writes it on our hearts
And shows inside how best to live it now

So He wrote it down in flame
and He wrote it on the world
Then he wrote it on the pages of our lives
But he wasn't finished yet,
he knew how hard that it could get
So He wrote it all down in his Holy book
so we wouldn't forget.

1 - Worship God

What is it you live for and all the world you'd give for;
what is it you trust to keep you strong
do you turn to strength or riches to get you through life's
glitches
or is it knowledge that you use to get along?

God's first command is worship him and worship him alone;
He made our hearts to long to turn to Him.
But make sure that your desire is fixed on what is higher
and the Devil isn't tempting you to sin.

Do you turn your back on grace, and put in the special place
reserved for Him some minor worldly love
or do you worship things as small as a poster on a wall
and forget to bow to Father God above.

Over The Waves

And what about your family or friends or food or fun
or do you love your work and leave your God ignored?
Do TV, sports and leisure form the passion in your heart?
What is it **you** put before the Lord?

2 - No Idols

To make God small is not at all a thing that we should do
And yet each day we try so many ways
In finite ways to replicate a God who's truly infinite,
to control and understand the thing we praise

God's second rule is not to make a fake to which to bow
though it be of him or any god at all
for creations by created Man his Creator cannot show
and our shoddy works, revealed to glory, pall.

An idol is not just of stone, we make them out of words
when we say that "this is God" and mean His whole
and the images we paint on the canvas of our mind
are bounded by the limits of our soul.

The tools and gifts he's given us are there for us to use
to help us understand some of his grace
but we're called away from earthly things
to join him in our hearts
and worship by his spirit not his face.

3 - God's Name

Some folks shout God's name when they're angry or in pain
and some use it in jokes so they seem clever
But do you shout, "Oh Daddy!" just 'cause things are going badly?
If not, then stop for love, 'cause God said **never**.

Over The Waves

And sometimes we pretend, to impress upon a friend
a holiness we do not really feel
but though we can gain fame, when we lie in Jesus name
God sees inside our hearts to what is real.

Is your weakness idle chat, or do you like to chew the fat
and throw scripture in to make a mooted gain
by abusing what is holy in an argument to solely
make a point, you bring dishonour to his name.

God's third law states it clearly, you must use his name so dearly,
for God's reputation from your witness grows
and the precious words of heaven
cannot come from lips of leaven –
and from salty words, no living water flows.

4 - Sabbath

In the busy world we live in, six days we are given
to do the work we need to earn our crust
and we must never shirk as we're called to kingdom work
to do the many things we need and must.

But the fourth of God's laws begs us take one day's pause
from quality time, not on whim
and to rest for a while from this world which defiles
and reflect on our friendship with Him.

So set aside one day, which may be a Sunday,
to worship to meditate and pray
but in your interaction, do not let distraction
or wandering thoughts draw you away

Over The Waves

Six days are set apart for body, mind and heart
this day is set to exercise your soul
for God won't have much to say to a spiritual couch potato
but holy Sabbath rest will keep us whole.

5 - Parents

You must honour your parents is rule number five
to inherit the gifts of the land
for family caring and brotherly sharing
is central to what God has planned

Do you honour your elders ahead on the road
and the wisdom that they pass along
or do old ways of thinking just get your heart sinking
so you have to convince them they're wrong.

And our fathers in government, how do they fare
Do you live by the laws they have set?
Which are the ones with which you disagree –
do you keep them or choose to forget?

Would you fight dishonour in your father's corner
or defend those you love to the last?
Are you ready to take for the great Father's sake
the abuse of this world but stand fast?

6 - Murder

To explain a bit further what he means by "don't murder"
(a thing that most folk would avoid)
It's rule number six that the Son Jesus picks
which we break by just getting annoyed.

Over The Waves

It's not just the doing that brings us to ruin
but the murderous thoughts in our mind
for the enemy's marks are the things of the dark
but God made us to love and be kind.

We are stabbed so much more by a word to the core
than by many a weapon of steel
though no blood can be seen where our assault has been
to our victim the injury's real.

And when we refrain from putting restraint
on those speaking with spiteful intent
We're as guilty as they, in the things that they say,
For we've given our tacit consent.

7 - Adultery

You may think that number seven
of the laws God gave from heaven
is reserved for those who share a marriage bed
it's about the bonds they make and the holy vows they take
when before the King of heaven they are wed.

The first meaning must be to turn from the lust
that would lead us to stray and to sin
but a meaning lies deeper for every law keeper
who chose to let God's Spirit in.

The law of pure life for husband and wife
should be born from a purity inside
and applies just the same to all in his name
for through Church we become Jesus bride.

Over The Waves

He makes it quite clear that there's just as severe
a betrayal of His wedding bed
that as much is at stake in the choices we make
and the things which we do in our head.

8 - Stealing

It's easy to say as you go through the day
that no way you'd contemplate stealing
and without hesitation you'd turn from temptation,
but would looking in truth be revealing?

That 'just a little time' on the company line
and the lunch break whose length you've abused
and the stationery taken – the eighth rule you're breaking
if you don't own the things you have used.

Or have you stolen men's truth by not sharing the proof
of God's love when they're standing in chains,
or seen them in need or imprisoned or starved
and offered but words for their pains.

Or do you steal from the Lord by reserving your best
and offering the half-gift of Cain –
are there times when you've promised your time and your tithe
and then claimed them for your use again?

9 - False Witness

The voice was made to praise the Ancient of all days
and to tell of all the wondrous things he's done
But turning on each other and slandering your brother
Is not a holy way to use your tongue.

Over The Waves

Do not malign is law number nine
love of self is where falsehood starts
when we lie without proof, the Spirit of Truth
is pushed to the corner of our hearts.

Your life stands a witness to that which you serve
and the world looks to see God in you
but there is nothing higher in the mind of a liar
so be sure people find truth in you.

10 - Envy

Do you want things that your neighbour has got
things he has or the way he is living?
well law number ten is about being content
with the lot in your life you've been given

Are your thoughts in the world as your fingers are curled
so tight around things which you own?
Is your life in God's hands or are you making plans
before Father God makes His will known?

The hopes which you have of a heavenly home
should suffice without seeking for more.
and if we have needs, in our prayers we should plead –
ask God's Spirit 'cause that's what he's for.

The A to Z of Outreach

A is for all, which is what we must give
as we ask Abba Father to help people live.
B is because he became one of us
when born as the Bethlehem baby, Jesus.
'C' how community grows in society
when as Christ's copies we gain notoriety.
Deep is the love he delivered for all
when he died to redeem us so no one need fall.
E is for-ever – his truth never ends -
as he's eager for each one to share with his friends.
F is for faithfulness unto the finish
for fishing of the fallen should never diminish.
G is the grace, which generates gifts
of gentle forgiveness for closing all rifts.
H is the happiness on heaven's part
when you are the hero that heals someone's heart.
I's the inside you must show round about
to intrigue and inspire and inside-people-out.
J is for Jesus who justified men
and just as he joined us, now we should join them.
K is for knowledge – he knows more than we
and kindles our kindness for strangers we see.
'L' is a place we don't want folk to go
so let's help them live freely by telling them so.
'M'-agine what we may manage to make
of this mad, mad world when His mercy we take.

Over The Waves

Never leave nameless the unnumbered faces
who just need a neighbour to win heaven's places.
Open your heart and open your mind;
in others such opulent treasure you'll find.
P is for patience, persistence and peace;
keep praying and trusting for prisoners' release.
The 'Q' is for heaven, as we quietly pull
by our questing, the narrower road will be full.
R we reliable and are we real?
We rescue by revealing the truth that we feel.
'S'-timate how many souls God can save
when we step out, surrender ourselves and be brave.
Take a good look at the times you are tested;
we tell a sad tale if by temptation we're bested.
U are the one called to serve Him today,
unconditionally, unreservedly under His sway.
Y's because yesterday He died to rise;
yield your heart to His calling and he'll make you 'wise'.
Z kingdom iz waiting true zealots to zee;
God zends Hiz diziples – who'z zat – You and Me.

He Did Not Come (Isaiah 53)

He did not come that we'd believe in Him
but because he believed in us
He didn't walk for praise to Calvary
but bore the sins of nations willingly

Surely our infirmities he took upon himself
and carried all our sorrows to the cross
He was pierced for our transgressions
crushed there for our sins
the pain that brought us peace was upon him

We like sheep had gone astray
each had turned to his own way
By his wounds we are healed
through his willing sacrifice.

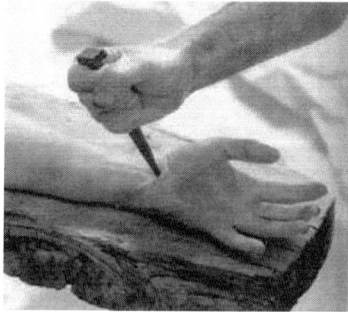

I Wish I Was God's Pencil

(This was a challenge title given to me by my housegroup)

I wish I was God's pencil
The utensil of his hand
He'd guide me through the stencil
Of the words that he had planned

Safe in the Master's true grip
With his hand upon my shoulder
He would not let my point slip,
I could be a little bolder

It would make a good impression
To be Holy Spirit led
When scribing my confession
And invoking what he's said

He would choose words of wonder
With which my point to cram
And would hone me for the task
Of giving glory to the Lamb

I would yield to him my service
And pray that he would find
An instrument of authority
And extension of his mind

The words that would pass through me
When following my ruler
Could be wrought into a kingdom crown
Scribed with diamonds by a jeweller

Over The Waves

What kind of pencil would I be
To write upon God's page
Not ultra trendy or cleverly bendy
But a prophet for my age

I may be willing hearted
To be seen as Heaven's fool
But I fail before I've started
Unless God's hand guides the tool

He sends his Holy Spirit
And I pray he'll keep me sharp
With such words as inspired David
And such muse as strung his harp

Without God, my gifting's pointless
Heavy handed and anointless
But when my author is my anchor
I can challenge this world's canker

And as the artist through his craft
Makes me the centre of his frame,
To draw the lost through his reflection,
Through his grace I'll do the same

For if I'm doing my job
While the Master is drawing me
I'll be drawing his hand back again
For all the world to see

Over The Waves

Those who serve for revelation
Have a duty to take care
That their precious inspiration
Is not tainted by life's care

God's instruments responsibly
Should steer from sin's oration
It is our call to write with love
And not with indignation

And it's not what I can do for him
That earns a jot of praise
But that in spite of my mistakes
His mercy can erase

And sometimes through a broken point
He speaks with greater grace
Than a copperplate or calligraphic
Render of his case

With harder lines and softer shades
He supports my human failings
To infuse his Spirit, challenge wrongs
And counter critics railings

I've wished to be his implement
Since the day my walk began
And there are days he convinces me
That maybe I already am.

For I've wished to be God's pencil
As if yet to be achieved
But I have been his instrument
From the day that I believed

Over The Waves

Engraven with the name of God
Submitting all myself
My perfect role to write, not gather
Dust upon the shelf

So when God has a task and asks,
It's not for chalk and slate
Nor special quill, nor pen ornate
He'd just ask "Where's my Kate"

And when the time for writing's through
And words are all confessed
The loving God who'll choose my end
Will lay my gift to rest

Thenceforth, in wordless worship
Freed from all the sins I've sinned,
I'll be diffused into His holiness
Like graphite on the wind.

Cry

When does persevering finish
When will it be broken
When will there be an end
To testing, when be rest?
Tears are my food -
Again you bring me to the well
The veil of tears.
When is it for me?
The darkness seeps into me
Through the open wounds I cannot see.
Where is the healing you promised?
Why am I so far from you?
Will there ever be a day I can look
And say it is good?
To feel the freedom from the darkness.
Oh Lord, how can I serve you
A broken thing, lost to joy?
Where has it gone? - the presence
Of you in my life.
I am so hungry for that
Which I have lost
Or maybe never had.
But I do not believe it is a lie
That I have known you.

Over The Waves

I will press on
I will not fall
I take up my shield
I take up your promises
I will not surrender to the foe.

My Salvation,
The name of Jesus has power
To heal.
Lord I pray for my healing
I pray this broken spirit
Can one day believe in Love
Can one day overcome.

Tears are still my food
Brokenness my bread
Oh Lord conquer that which is in me
Whatever stands between us
Break it down.

I Have Stood Upon the Mountain

I have stood upon your mountain
Felt the wonder of your grace
I have drunk there of your fountain
I have sought your hidden face
I have breathed in awe and wonder
A communion so profound
With the world around me fading
I have knelt on Holy Ground

Now send me out to the desert
Let me walk along the plains
Speaking of salvation
In the voice of him who reigns
Let me go with your message
To the lost man in the street
But let me never shake the dust
Of the holy mountain from my feet

Over The Waves

In the middle of the desert
I have found the holy spring
Where the river of Salvation love
Brings life to everything
And into Man's weary heart of dust
Sweet peace and mercy flow
An oasis of God's still small voice
In the place Acacias grow

Now send me out to the chaos
With the healing balm of grace
And a hand upon my shoulder
And a sweet heart to embrace
As a pitcher for your spirit
And prophet for our times
Leaving footprints of forever
In the dust of Man's designs.

Lead Me From The Place of Selfish Dreams

Lead me from the place of selfish dreams
Lead me from the place of pride
Lead me from the place of comfort
Till we reach the other side
And I know if you are with me
Nothing can go wrong
In the circumstance if I'm in your plans
Your love will keep me strong
And you'll calm the wind and waters
If I'll only raise my hands
For you save your sons and daughters
From the failure of their stands
And I know that if I'm open
To your presence as I pray
The distant shore I can barely see
May be just a simple breath of prayer away.

The Mother of Nations

The Mother of Nations who was she?
Just like God or just like me?

When God made Eve he chose to start
With bone of Adam from his heart,
No lesser cleaving than the one
That cleaves the Father to the Son.
He broke the gate to solitude
And with the breath of life imbued
That stern protector of the heart
With strength to bear a suffrage part.

A graceful wife he honed to sup
Equal handed from His cup,
So Adam and his gentler part
Could share the cleft beneath His heart.
Yet even from that trysting gate
Of heart to heart, the woman ate
And fruit, forbidden, from her hand
Brought desolation to the land.

Over The Waves

With eyes of guilt and hearts of shame
And thoughts which minds should not contain
The poison of that nectar sweet
Makes clean hearts fear their God to meet -
Whose innocence, broached with restraint,
Submits their seed to equal taint
And in the hinterland, now lost,
Condemned they sup the nectar's cost.

A graceless god would their disgrace
Delete and craft anew his face
But He who all the world designs
In banishment new fitness finds
And to the one who tore his heart
Gives grace to make a kingdom start -
A line unbroken through the womb
To herald in His empty tomb.

Through blood and bone inviolate
The promise of His presence great
The Word, through seed of sinful man
And mother's flesh will seal God's plan.
Till maiden's sweetness sacrosanct
By ardent Spirit's touch is thanked
And true redemption's infant qualms
Seek comfort in a mother's arms

Over The Waves

Nestled there beneath her breast
The wealth of heaven's grace is pressed -
True absolution stamped in flesh
Begins the walk of Man afresh
And God's own heritage becomes
The dower of a thousand mums
Whose nurture through the wasteland age
Sustained His Word upon Man's page.

Faultless bride or faithless flaw
Through whom God's mercy shows in awe
Her splinters of the Father's grace
From Mother church now fill this place.
Since from the dross of offence gleamed
The Mothered race of Man redeemed,
Our God extends his hand in trust
Against accusation in the dust.

And deeper now than nature's grace
He shows each heart His hidden face.
The chiefest arrow to his bow
To pierce our outer skins of woe
Is she who from our tender birth
Breeds ardent spirits here on earth
For lovely, plain, sublime or odd
She's the mother heart of Father God.

All The Words Have Been Said

All the words have been said before
And all the music played
There's nothing left that I can call my own
My voice is stilled within.
In my soul a wild surrender
Strives with a wilder grace beyond my grasp
Yet stilled in breathless bliss of knowing
This intimate invader of my life.

Deeper than my deep, you have called me
To a purpose, beyond my vision's sky,
Lord, be the centre of my praises
True everlasting height of all my heights.
Fragment my weak illusions
And lead me through the shards
To the still point of your being –
The holy sanctuary of your heart.

Over The Waves

Enfold me in the arms of the Eternal
Suffuse me in your ever-fathomed-depths.
As when you knit me, deep within my Mother
Cradle me, complete, to heaven's breast.
Let Your will become my spirit's spring-source
My inmost being to Your utmost draw
Overwhelm this lost world's smaller loving
To captive grace my errant soul restore.

Do you know how much I love you
O glorious source of all my days
Indwell me with transcending love
Till grace erases all that is
From Time's disgrace, lead me to waters clear
To shed the cloying dust of life
And cast aside the painful thorns and chains,
Trade rags of shame for robes of white.

Yet still all words are dust - insubstantial,
Imperfect vision impotent to see
The incandescent lightning which surrounds you
Ineffable, eternal dignity.
And still all acts are cheap, tawdry, undone -
Overshadowed, weighed as wanting by the One
Whose once and only sanguine gift to all
Our Sin surmounts, atoning Adam's fall.

Over The Waves

There is nothing I can bring that is new
But a new commitment to kneel at your feet
And the pain and joy of each new day
Seems a sacrifice too easy to pay
For between you and me
Is communion so deep
That words cannot fathom
A silent heart beat
An invading song of glory
That coruscates my heart
Enervating every action
And suffusing every part

No ear can know such music in this place
No human heart-in-heart such breathless grace.

Dedication

Every Christian's walk is blessed by many other voices, too many to mention here. However I would like to acknowledge the names of the six men of God who have so far been my Pastors and Mentors. Through their dedication and lives of service, they have shown me what it is to be a servant of God, and through their support and significant words they have helped me to find what it means to be a child of God.

My prayer is that God continues to work through their ministries and continues to bless them on their ongoing walk with Him.

They are:
ANDY MACLEAN

BRIAN GILL

ALAN PRICE

CHRIS BOWATER

MATTHEW COOPER

ROBIN BAKER

And finally to the seventh, who is the man from whom all came and to whom all belongs – the man who is God and the ruler of my heart. I pray that these twenty years have only been the beginning and that the road ahead will bear much more fruit. He is my Past, Present and Future – He is all my gifting and all my grace. He is:

YESHUA — GOD'S SALVATION

His Forever - Mine Forever

Over The Waves

Copyright Statement

All poems in this book are copyrighted to the author Mad Doodle
(a.k.a K.J.Sutcliffe). The author authorises the reproduction and
performance of any of the poetry and sketches for any non-profit
church, outreach or social use, so long as their use is in
accordance with scripture and bears no direct or implied
detriment to the name or person of the God which they honour.

For any commercial interest in any of the poems/sketches, please
contact Mad Doodle at the address below. The author is
currently seeking an agent for these and other Christian and
secular poems and would appreciate any professional interest.

Please also Email to encourage the author if any of the works in
this book touch you personally or if you have found them useful
in your churches.

Share the harvest

The intention is that profits for this publication will be used in
support of the two causes on the following page. If you have felt
blessed or challenged by anything or if you have used any items for
broader outreach, please consider making a contribution to one or
both of these projects.

The author would also be happy for proceeds for this work to support
other worthy charities. If you have a Christian network or feel you
may be able to sell copies of this book within your own churches, on-
demand copies can be made available to you at a reasonable price
and you can market them at whatever you feel appropriate in support
of your charity. Please contact the author for prices, with details of
the charity/church.

Disclaimer

Liability for all the views expressed in and contents of this book is the
author's and no liability lies with the publishers, the charities
supported or those in the dedication.

Contact: mad.doodle@googlemail.com

http://www.oasischristiancentre.org.uk

Oasis Christian Centre is the church at which I am a member. We are currently pursuing what we believe to be the will of God in replacing our church building, which thanks to God's blessing is currently too small for us to meet in.
Please visit the website to get an idea of the number of community ministries in the church which will be made possible by this project and consider if you could support it.

HOPE AND KINDNESS
http://hopeandkindness.org

Hope and Kindness is an orphanage charity set up by (extra)ordinary people who saw a need and stepped up to meet it. From their own busy lives they dedicate hours of time and other resources to bring meaningful, supported lives to many young people in the desperately resourceless land of Kenya.
Please visit their website and consider either a donation or one-to-one support of one of these beautiful, God-loved children.

151

The Lord bless you and keep you--
the Lord make His face shine upon you,
and be gracious unto you;
the Lord lift up His countenance upon you,
and give you peace.

Numb. 6:24-26.